30 MORE PLANES FOR THE PAPER PILOT

30 MORE PLANES FOR THE PAPER PILOT

Peter Vollheim

POCKET BOOKS

New York   London   Toronto   Sydney   Tokyo

An *Original* Publication of POCKET BOOKS

 POCKET BOOKS, a division of Simon & Schuster Inc.
1230 Avenue of the Americas, New York, NY 10020

ISBN: 0-671-65810-7

First Pocket Books trade paperback printing December 1988

10 9 8 7 6 5 4 3 2 1

POCKET and colophon are trademarks of
Simon & Schuster Inc.

Printed in the U.S.A.

This is for my son, Weston Chance Vollheim.

ACKNOWLEDGMENTS

During my seemingly never-ending prison years in school, one course that I enjoyed and have used in daily life was mechanical drawing, taught by Mr. Val Green. That was back in 1967 at Curis Junior High, Sudbury, Massachusetts. In fact, that was the only course in which I ever received an A. I still have my drawings from that school year with Mr. Green—the only work that I saved from my school years. The skills I acquired from Mr. Green I have used to create not only the line drawings in this book, but those in my two previous books on paper airplanes as well. I have retained and used everything Mr. Green taught me, right down to rolling the pencil when drawing a ruled line to retain a sharp point on the pencil. Thank you, Mr. Green.

My co-workers, Bill, Paulette, and Angela deserve a round of applause for putting up with the paper airplane strafing attacks that occur on occasion during the testing phases of these designs.

My heartfelt thanks go to Les Longworth, who has been a good friend for many years and has used his somewhat warped sense of humor and marvelous talent to create the sketches for this book.

My gratitude goes to my editor, Sally Peters, for her patience, understanding, and assistance in the preparation of this book.

Thanks go to Jonathan Hill and his lovely wife Lillian for allowing me to invade their home and set up my base of operations in their living room, and for tolerating massed kamikaze flights whenever I visit New York.

I am grateful to Jonathan Hill and Mike Krinke of J & M Studio for furnishing me with all the required photographs and for going the extra mile during the weekend photo marathon.

My love goes to my best friend and wife, Paulette Marie Armstrong Vollheim. Her determination and working spirit, which I have imitated, and her encouragement are responsible for all of my accomplishments, past and future.

INTRODUCTION

This book is the flip side of my previous paper airplane book *30 Planes for the Paper Pilot,* hence the name *30 More Planes for the Paper Pilot.* The first book dealt with airplanes made out of sheets of paper, and it contained a few composite designs (airplanes constructed from plastic drinking straws, paper, index cards, and business cards). This book deals primarily with composite designs, but it also contains some traditional genuine paper designs. The reasons for this are many. Composite designs offer higher performance, are more aerodynamic, and are more varied. Also, there are almost no other books about these designs.

The composite aircraft in this book are unusually efficient. Because index cards are strong and razor thin, they make highly effective airfoils. And with index cards, you can adjust the leading-edge slats and trailing edge flaps. Index-cards also allow quick production of this type of aircraft. You can stack the wings, tail surfaces, and other parts while you are cutting. In this fashion, you can quickly produce an entire air armada.

Plastic straws, the other basic building material used in these designs, are strong, light in weight, easily available, and best of all, cheap.

The last three designs in this book represent a large step up in paper airplane technology. These airplanes use easy tab-in-slot assembly that ensures proper wing-tail incidence, and their construction is light, strong, and quite foolproof. They are copies of today's jet fighters: McDonnell Douglas' F-15 Eagle, McDonnell Douglas' F/A 18 Hornet, and Northrop's F-20 Tigershark. The wings and tail surfaces of these three airplanes are in scale to each other. Due to the relatively high wing loadings (small wings), fighters don't have the glide ratio of some of the other airplanes, but they are very stable and are terrific fliers.

For all non–aviation orientated types, who aren't interested in the mechanics of how or why a plane flies, I suggest skimming Chapters 1 and 2 and moving right along to the airplane-building instructions, which begin in Chapter 3. I have made countless paper airplanes. My office is literally snowed under with paper airplanes. I have even made airplanes out of heavy aluminum foil, and they fly beautifully. I have large and dusty boxes of paper airplane designs.

Basically they fall into three categories. Some are incredible fliers but require intricate and tedious assembly. Others, while easy to fabricate and great looking, fly like a one-winged duck and require many aerodynamic add-ons and constant tuning to fly properly. The aircraft in this book, however, are the very best of eagles. They are easy-to-construct, true performance fliers.

30 MORE
PLANES
FOR THE
PAPER PILOT

2

WINGS

Wings come in all shapes and sizes. Each design is specialized in one aspect of flight, but few are good in all phases. The classic delta-winged paper airplane is certainly the top choice for strength, ease of fabrication, and acceptable flight characteristics through all speed ranges. And luckily a sheet of paper lends itself perfectly to the building of a delta wing. However, if slow flight is your cup of tea, then a higher aspect ratio wing (longer) would be a better choice for you. Generally, the more wingspan an airplane has, the more slowly and docilely it will fly. Conversely, the less wingspan it has, the faster and more maneuverable it will be.

In this book you will find patterns for delta, LEX delta, swept, diamond, constant cord, and tapered wings. My personal favorite is the LEX delta wing. This configuration has the best compromise of docile stall characteristics and high-speed stability, because of the triangular strakes or chine that precede the wing itself. This produces a vortex of air that swirls over the wing near the stall point, and smooths out the airflow, prolonging the burbling that reduces the stall speed.

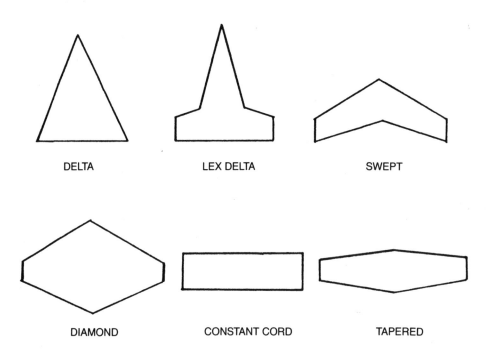

DELTA   LEX DELTA   SWEPT

DIAMOND   CONSTANT CORD   TAPERED

Generally, LEX delta, delta, and constant cord wings have the best stall characteristics. LEX delta and delta wings also happen to have some of the best high-speed characteristics as well. They are the logical choice for a "do it all" paper airplane.

Tapered wings, wings that taper toward the tip are the most efficient if you want the least amount of drag and the best glide. Swept-back wings, similar to jet airliner wings, are very efficient

and that it requires a level launch. In a nose-down attitude, launch the airplane with a gentle motion, and release it so that you don't put any spin on it that will affect its flight. Some of the airplanes in this book are very unconventional and require a rather unorthodox hold.

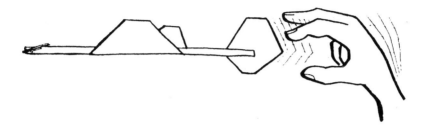

Of course you are not limited to these launching techniques. They are only presented as guidelines.

6

GRADUATION

   I have included a technical data block for each airplane in this book. Those of you who are interested in aerodynamics can compare the wing span and weight of the various models. Once you are familiar with these two values and what they refer to, you will be able to tell how an airplane will fly even before the first flight. Below are two sketches to help you familiarize yourself with the parts of a paper airplane.

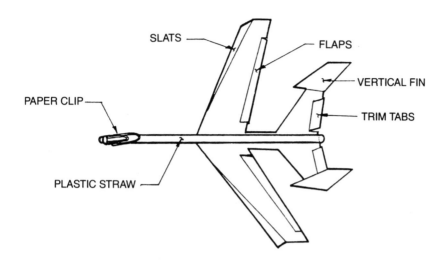

SLATS

FLAPS

VERTICAL FIN

PAPER CLIP

TRIM TABS

PLASTIC STRAW

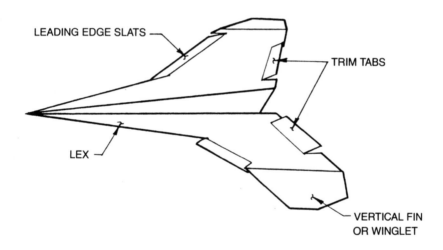

LEADING EDGE SLATS

TRIM TABS

LEX

VERTICAL FIN
OR WINGLET

DESIGN *1*

TYPE: pronounced delta
WINGSPAN: $6\frac{5}{8}''$
LENGTH: $14''$
WEIGHT: 6.1 grams

PILOT REPORT

This is an elongated version of Design #1 in my other book, *30 Planes for the Paper Pilot*. The increased length gives this airplane more inertia, enabling it to perform superbly outdoors. The large wing area and low weight give the airplane terrific slow flight and good glide. The delta wing and long length provide excellent stability at high speed.

MATERIALS REQUIRED

 1 8½″ × 14″ sheet of paper
 cellophane tape
 ruler
 razor blade

1A) Fold the sheet of paper in half lengthwise.

1B) Fold the corners as shown.

1C) Fold the corners again to ⅝″ from the end.

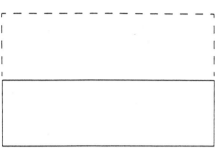

1D) Open the sheet and lay it flat.

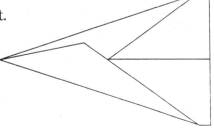

1E) Fold the sheet in half along the center crease, fold over the tang, and tape it.

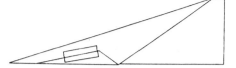

1F) Measure 1¼″ from the center crease at the tail and fold the wings along the diagonal line to the nose.

1G) Fold the leading edge slats approximately 1″.

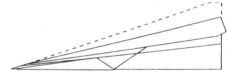

1H) Cut the trim tabs to the dimensions shown (⅜, ⅝). Position the wing dihedral, leading edge slats, and trim tabs as shown in the photograph.

DESIGN 2

TYPE: delta
WINGSPAN: 7¼″
LENGTH: 6″
WEIGHT: 3.8 grams

PILOT REPORT

This is a classic delta paper airplane with excellent slow- and moderate-speed performance. The high camber wing produces a great deal of lift, the result being a very efficient design with an excellent flat glide.

MATERIALS REQUIRED

1 8½″ × 11″ sheet of paper
cellophane tape
ruler
razor blade

2A) Fold the sheet of paper in half lengthwise.

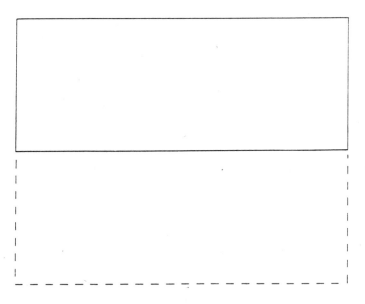

2B) Measure 3⅜″ along the upper surface and cut along the diagonal line as shown.

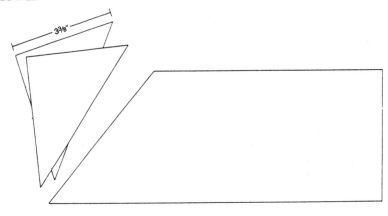

2C) Measure 2¼″ from the upper right corner and fold along the diagonal line to the nose.

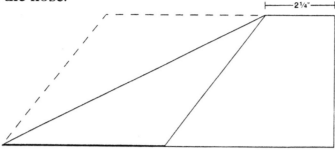

2D) Unfold the paper and lay it flat.

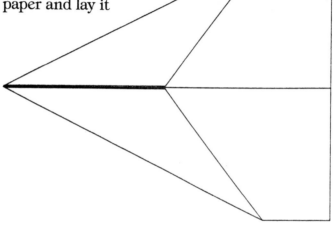

2E) Fold the nose over to a point 1⅛″ from the trailing edge.

2F) Fold the whole thing in half along the center crease.

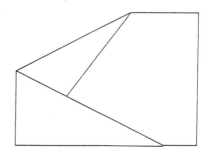

2G) Fold the leading edges over.

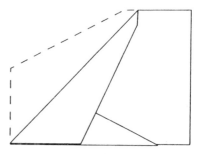

2H) Measure 1⅜″ from the center crease at the tail, and fold the wings along the diagonal line to the nose.

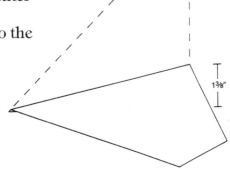

1⅜″

2I) Unfold the wings and fold the leading edge slats approximately 1½″. Tape the center section.

2J) Unfold the slats and cut the trim tabs as shown. Position the wing dihedral, leading edge slats, and trim tabs as shown in the photograph.

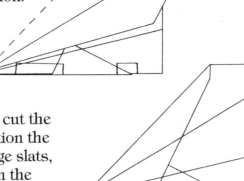

¼″

½″

TYPE: squared-tipped diamond
WINGSPAN: approximately 6″
LENGTH: 7¾″
WEIGHT: 4.2 grams

PILOT REPORT

This neat little diamond wing airplane can be flown indoors as well as out. This design performs best in moderate- to high-speed ranges due to its high wing loading.

MATERIALS REQUIRED

1 8½″ × 11″ sheet of paper
1 paper clip
cellophane tape
ruler
razor blade

3A) Cut the sheet of paper down to 8½″ × 8½″. Fold this square in half diagonally.

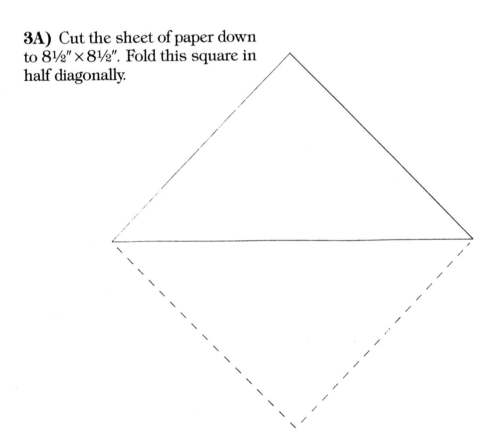

3B) Fold the corners to the center crease.

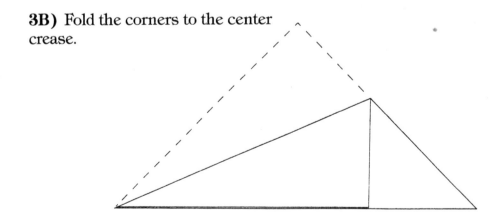

3C) Lay the paper flat with the center crease up.

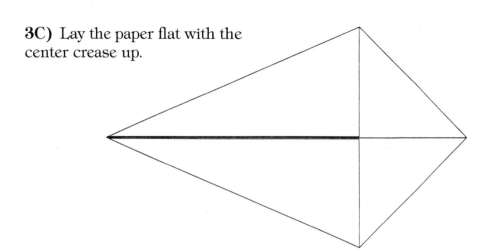

3D) Fold the nose over to the middle edge.

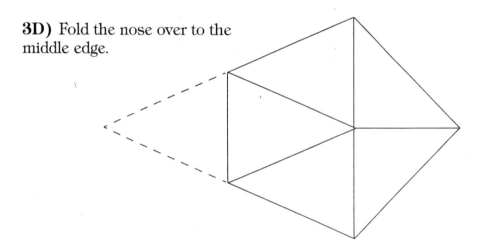

3E) Fold the whole thing in half along the center crease. Fold the front corners as shown.

3F) Measure 1½″ from the center crease at the tail and fold the wings along the diagonal line to the nose.

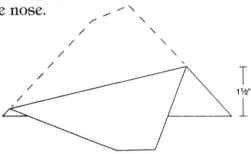

1½″

3G) Unfold the wings and fold the leading edge slats ¾″. Tape the center section as shown. Cut the trim tabs to the dimensions shown. Position the wing dihedral, leading edge slats, and trim tabs to the approximate positions shown in the photograph. Attach a paper clip to the nose.

¾″

¼″

½″

TYPE: diamond
WINGSPAN: 5¾"
LENGTH: 6½"
WEIGHT: 3.6 grams

PILOT REPORT

With its ultra-high wing loading and diamond configuration, this design is exceptional at high speed. If trimmed too nose-up (trim tabs too high) for slower flight, however, it will become unstable in pitch.

1 8½″ × 11″ sheet of paper
cellophane tape
ruler
razor blade

4A) Cut the paper down to 8½″ × 8½″. Fold this square in half diagonally.

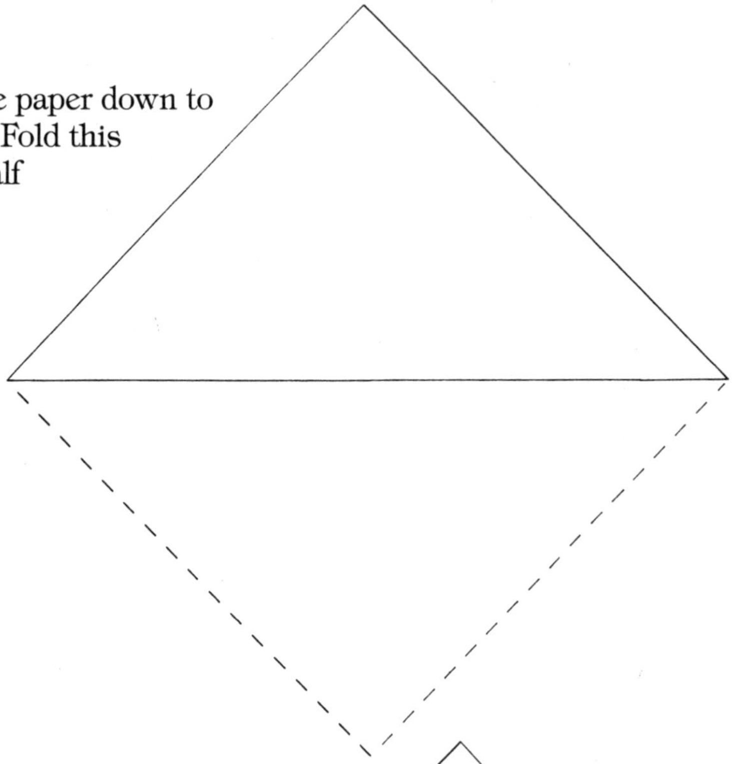

4B) Lay the paper flat with the crease up. Fold over one corner 3⅝″.

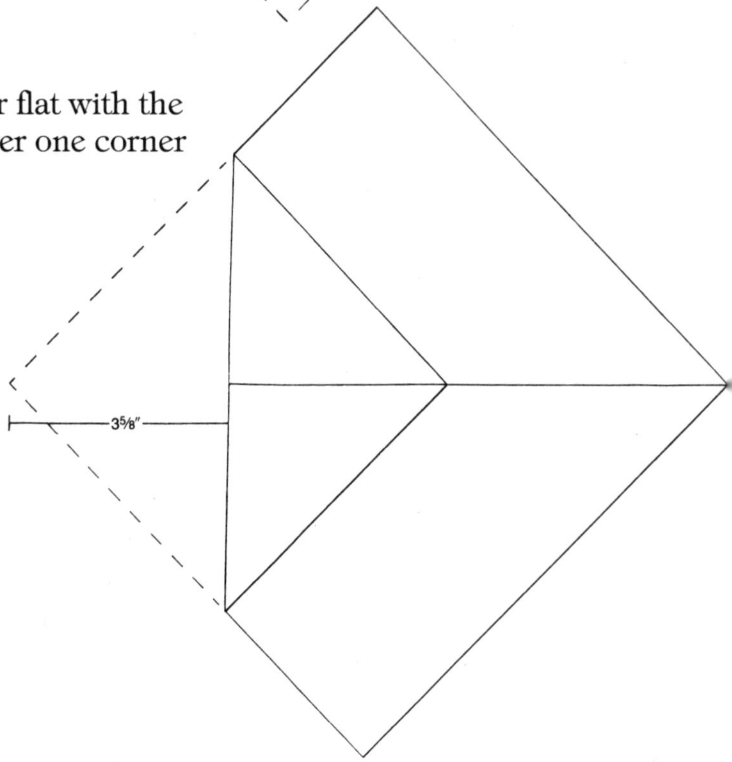

3⅝″

4C) Fold the corners again to the center crease.

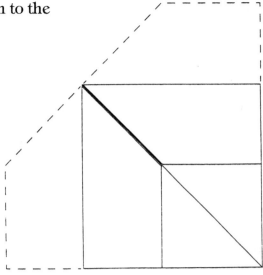

4D) Fold the nose over approximately 1¾".

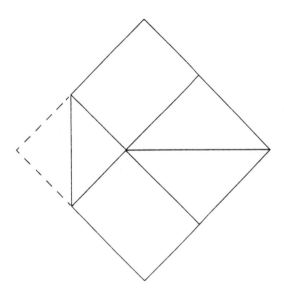

4E) Fold in half along the center crease.

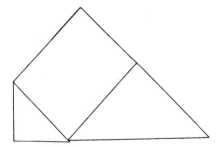

4F) Fold the leading edges back to the center crease. Tape the center section as shown.

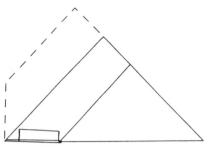

4G) Measure 1⅜″ from the center crease at the tail. Fold the wings along the diagonal line to the nose.

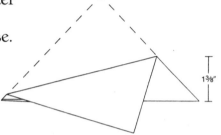

4H) Fold the leading edge slats ⅝″ at the tip. Cut the trim tabs to the dimensions shown. Position the wing dihedral, leading edge slats, and trim tabs in the approximate position shown in the photograph.

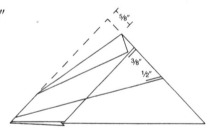

TYPE: LEX delta
WINGSPAN: approximately 7⅜"
LENGTH: 7"
WEIGHT: 4.7 grams

PILOT REPORT

This is a "do it all"—excellent through all speed ranges, good for indoor as well as outdoor flight, easy to build and fly. This is the result of the LEX delta design.

MATERIALS REQUIRED

1 8 ½" × 11" sheet of paper
cellophane tape
ruler
razor blade

GA) Fold the sheet of paper in half lengthwise.

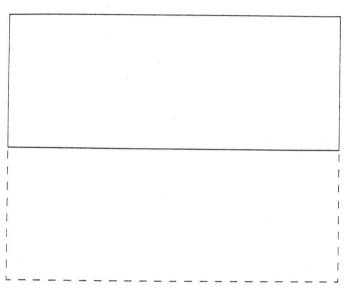

6B) Fold the corners as shown.

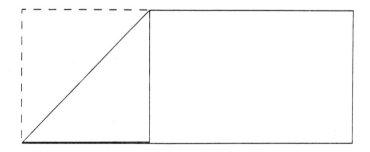

6C) Fold the corners again to ⅝" from the center crease.

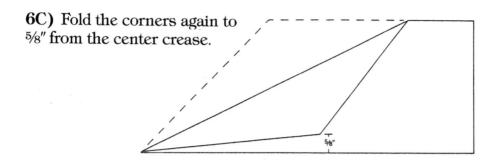

6D) Open the paper on a flat surface.

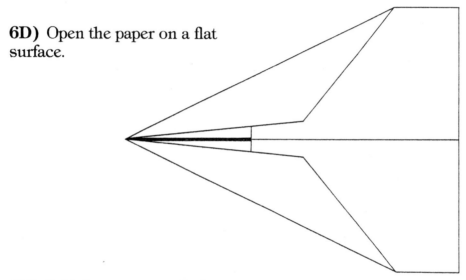

6E) Fold the nose over 6 ¾".

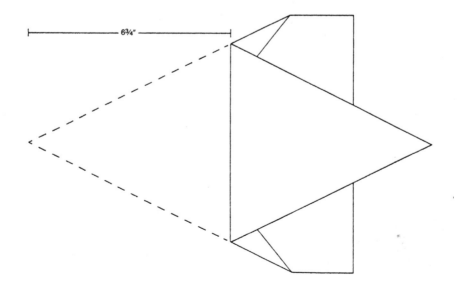

6F) Fold the nose back over 4 ¾".

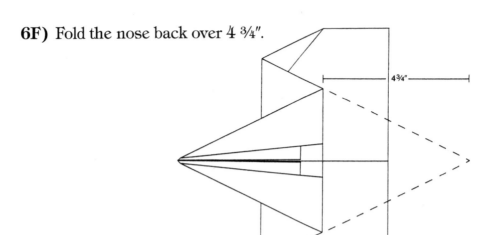

6G) Fold the paper in half along the center crease.

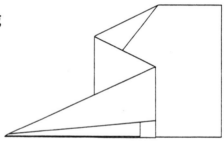

6H) Fold the corners and tape them as shown.

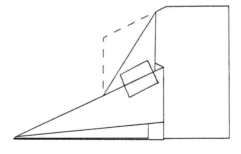

MATERIALS REQUIRED

1 8 ½″ × 11″ sheet of paper
1 paper clip
pencil
cellophane tape
ruler
razor blade

7A) Fold the sheet of paper in half widthwise.

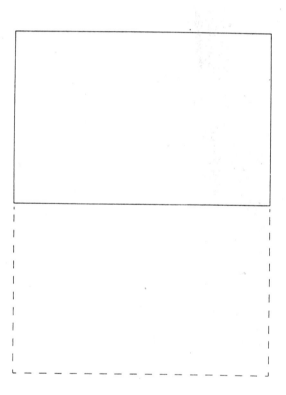

7B) Cut off the corners opposite the center crease to the dimensions shown.

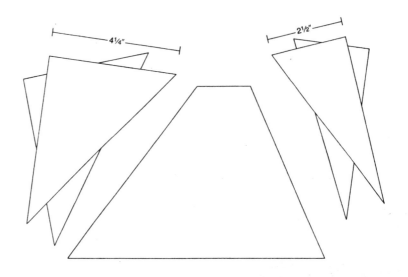

7C) On the left side make a pencil mark at 6". On the right side make a mark at 3¾". Cut off the end on a diagonal line connecting these two marks.

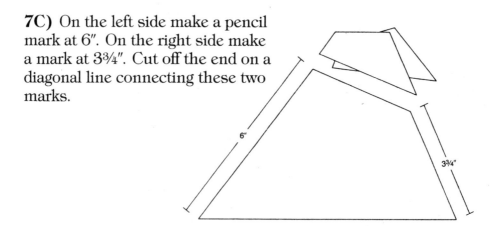

7D) Fold the corners as shown.

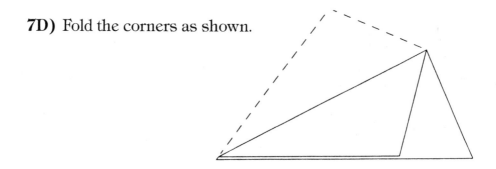

7E) Open the paper and lay it out flat.

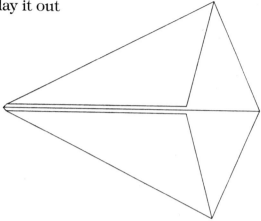

7F) Fold the nose over 4 ⅞".

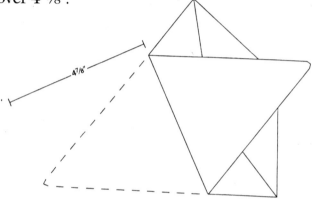

7G) Fold the nose back 1 ¼" from the previous fold.

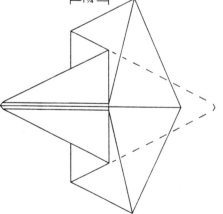

7H) Fold the corners as shown.

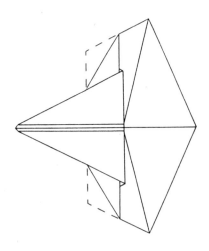

7I) Fold the paper in half along the center crease and tape the previously folded corners as shown.

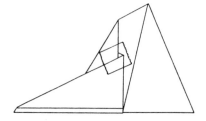

7J) Measure 1 ¼″ from the center crease at the tail and fold the wings along a diagonal line to the nose.

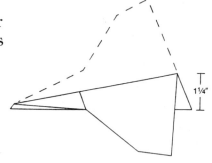

7K) Unfold the wings. Fold the leading edge slats approximately ¾″ and cut the trim tab. Position the wings, slats, and trim tabs as shown in the photograph. Attach a paper clip to the nose.

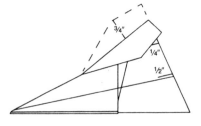

8

TYPE: LEX delta with winglets
WINGSPAN: 6¾"
LENGTH: 6"
WEIGHT: 5.3 grams

PILOT REPORT

This is a great little airplane. It is very stable due to relatively highly loaded LEX delta. The winglets provide a measurable amount of added lift and stability. This design is excellent for indoor as well as outdoor flying in the moderate- to high-speed range.

1 8½″×11″ sheet of paper
1 paper clip
cellophane tape
ruler
razor blade

8A) Fold the sheet of paper in half
lengthwise.

8B) Fold the corners as shown.

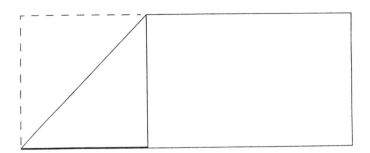

8C) Fold the corners again as shown.

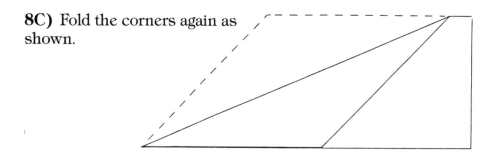

8D) Open the paper and lay it flat with the center crease up.

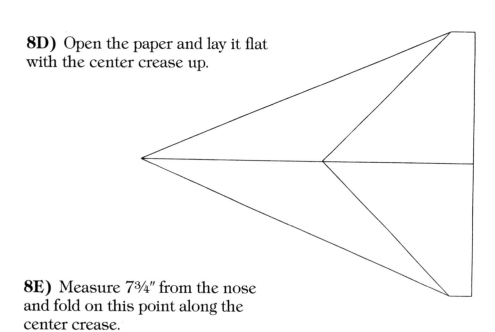

8E) Measure 7¾" from the nose and fold on this point along the center crease.

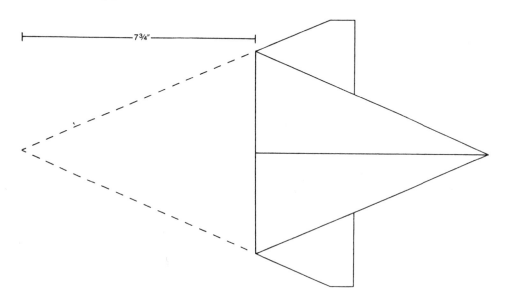

8F) Measure 5⅛″ from the nose and fold again.

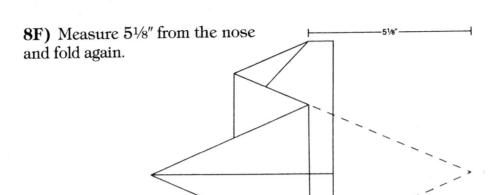

8G) Fold the outside corners inward.

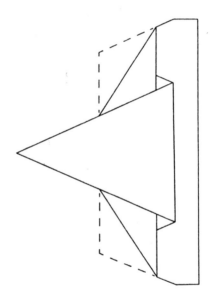

8H) Fold the paper in half along the center crease. Tape the previously folded corners.

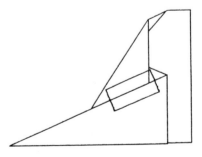

8I) Measure 1¼″ from the center crease and fold the wings on a diagonal line to the nose.

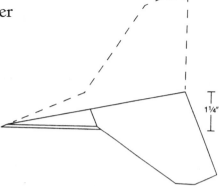

8J) Unfold the wings and fold the winglet/twin vertical fins approximately ⅞″, noting the canted angle. Cut the leading edge slats as shown.

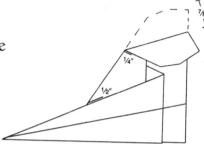

8K) Fold the leading edge slats. Cut the trim tabs to the dimensions shown. Position the trim tabs, slats, and winglets as shown in the photograph. Attach a paper clip to the nose.

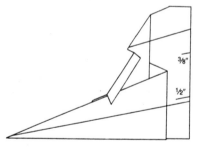

TYPE: conventional tail delta
WINGSPAN: $7\frac{3}{4}''$
LENGTH: $7\frac{7}{8}''$
WEIGHT: 6.8 grams

PILOT REPORT

This design is definitely something different, utilizing a delta wing with a conventional tail and trim tabs. This design is best used for outdoor flight.

1 8½″ × 11″ sheet of paper
4 paper clips
ruler
razor blade

9A) Fold one corner of the sheet
of paper as shown.

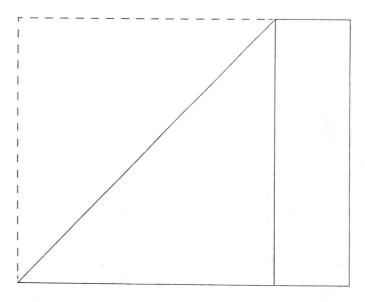

9B) Unfold that corner and fold
the opposite corner in the same
manner.

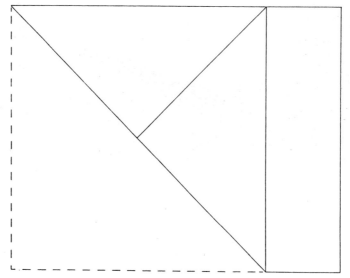

9C and 9D) Unfold and refold along the creases to end up with two folds inside as illustrated in step 9D.

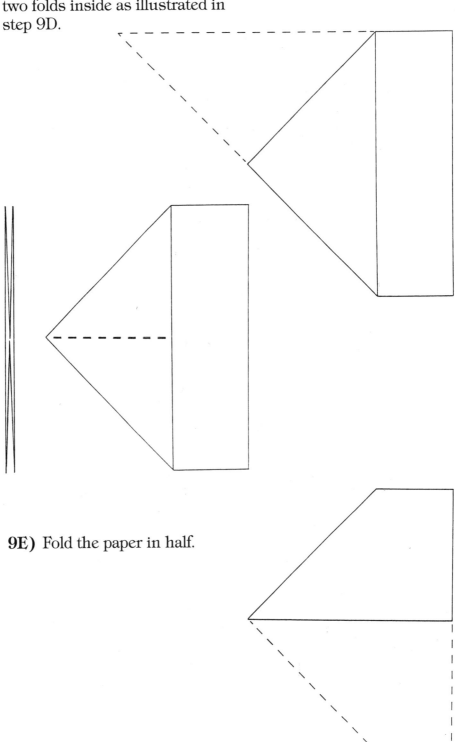

9E) Fold the paper in half.

9F) Lay the paper flat with the smooth surface up.

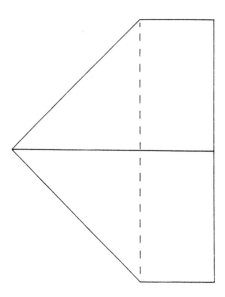

9G) Leaving the bottom triangle undisturbed, fold the upper section toward the center crease. Tape the surfaces as shown.

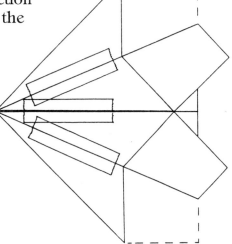

9H) Fold the paper in half.

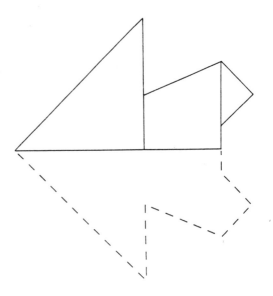

9I) Fold the wings as shown.

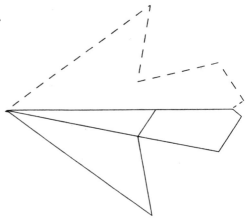

9J) Unfold wings and lay flat as shown. Fold the leading edge slats even with the edge. Make a cut approximately ¾" long at the trailing edge for the trim tabs. Position the leading edge slats, wings, and trim tabs as shown in the photograph. Attach four paper clips to the nose.

TYPE: delta
WINGSPAN: 8¼"
LENGTH: 5¾"
WEIGHT: 5.7 grams

PILOT REPORT

This is a design for people who enjoy something a little different. This one uses paper clips for trim—three for indoor flight and four for high apartment window flight. With four paper clips, the airplane excels in high-speed flight, because it gets more stable with increased speed. Manufacture this design in large quantities and launch the planes from a rooftop or bridge.

MATERIALS REQUIRED

1 8½″ × 11″ sheet of paper
3 or 4 paper clips
cellophane tape
ruler
razor blade

10A) Cut 2½″ from the sheet of paper to obtain a 8½″ × 8½″ square. Fold this square diagonally.

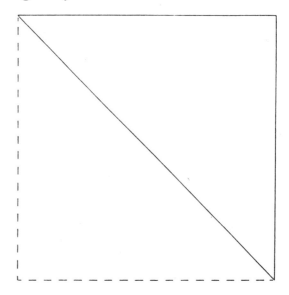

10B) Unfold the square and refold it the other way.

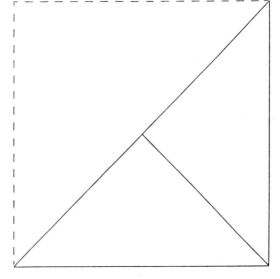

10C & 10D) Fold the sides in. An
end view is shown in step 10D.

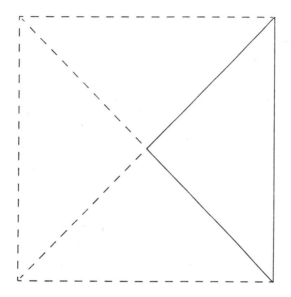

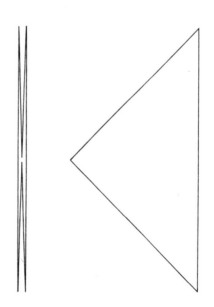

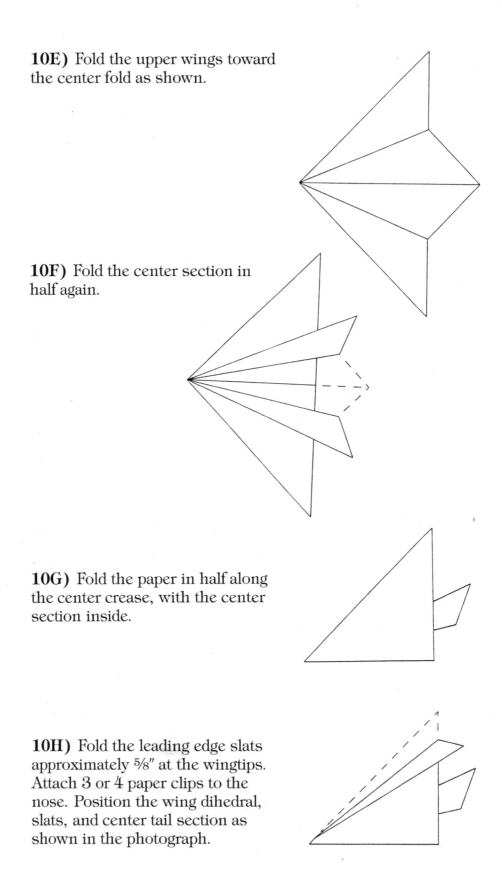

10E) Fold the upper wings toward the center fold as shown.

10F) Fold the center section in half again.

10G) Fold the paper in half along the center crease, with the center section inside.

10H) Fold the leading edge slats approximately ⅝″ at the wingtips. Attach 3 or 4 paper clips to the nose. Position the wing dihedral, slats, and center tail section as shown in the photograph.

TYPE: diamond
WINGSPAN: 11″
LENGTH: 5″
WEIGHT: 4.6 grams

PILOT REPORT

This is an interesting flapping-wing airplane. The design never fails to get a smile as the wings wave up and down during flight. Somewhat tricky to launch, but very efficient, this airplane should be launched with a slightly nose-up attitude. If it is launched incorrectly, this airplane will "tuck" and nose-dive. Properly handled, however, it is excellent for indoor as well as calm-weather outdoor flight.

MATERIALS REQUIRED

    1 8½″ × 11″ sheet of paper
    2 paper clips
    cellophane tape
    ruler
    razor blade

11A) Trim the sheet of paper to a
8½″ × 8½″ square.

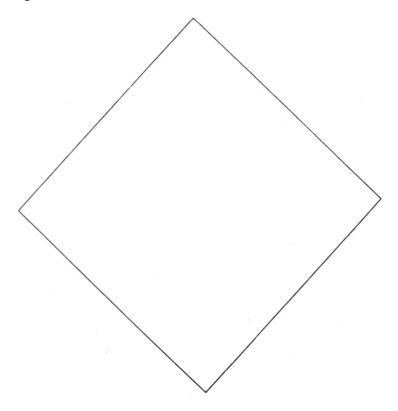

11B) Fold the square in half diagonally.

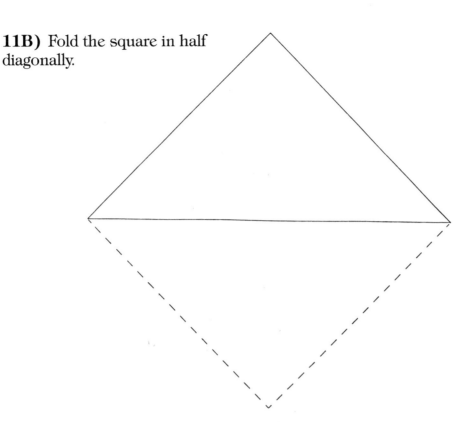

11C) Unfold the square and lay it flat with the crease up. Fold the next corner along the fold to a point 3¼″ from the corner.

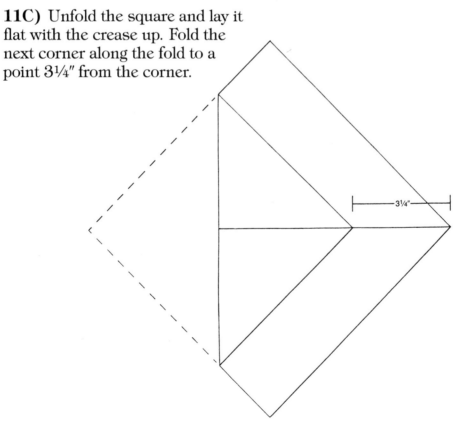

11D) Fold back the first fold again so that it is even with the two corners.

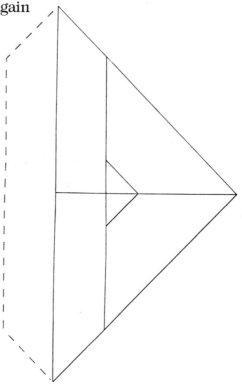

11E) Turn the paper over with the crease facing down.

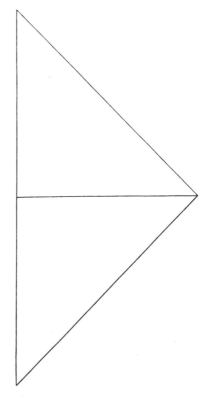

11F) Fold in half along the center crease.

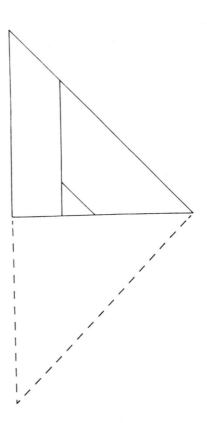

11G) Fold the wings 3″ from the bottom fold.

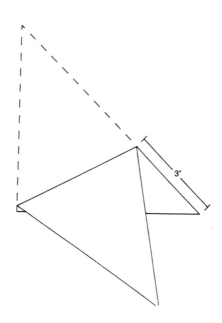

3″

11H) Unfold the wings. Cut the trim tabs and stabilizer fins to the dimensions shown. Cut off the aft point and tape the wing section as shown.

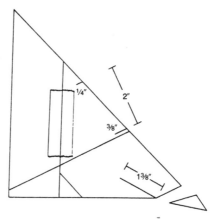

11I) Fold the leading edges slat ⅝″ at the wingtips. Fold the horizontal stabilizer fins up as shown, noting the canted angle. Place the wings, leading edge slats, stabilizer fins, and trim tabs in the approximate position shown in the photograph. Attach two paper clips to the nose.

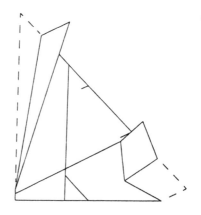

DESIGN *12*

TYPE: delta with winglets
WINGSPAN: 8″
LENGTH: 8⅛″
WEIGHT: 4.7 grams

PILOT REPORT

This design flies extremely well despite its simple construction and looks. With its large delta wing with winglets, it is a terrific flier in the slow- to moderate-speed ranges. Very stable and almost foolproof in fabrication, this airplane is one of the top designs in this book. Perfect for indoor as well as high apartment window flying.

MATERIALS REQUIRED

1 5″×8″ index card
1 plastic straw
1 paper clip
cellophane tape
ruler
razor blade

12A) Fold a 5″×8″ index card in half widthwise.

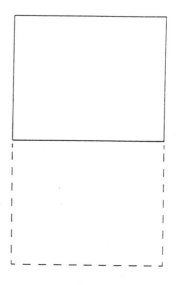

12B) Measure ½″ up from the center crease on the left side, and 1¾″ from the upper right. Cut along the diagonal line. Make two ½″ cuts for the trim tabs in the approximate location shown. Cut the winglets approximately 1¼″ from each wingtip as shown.

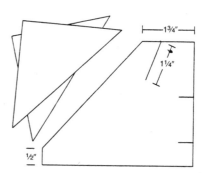

12C) Fold the leading edge slats back approximately ¼″. Fold the winglets as shown (note the canted angle).

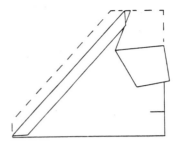

12D) Tape a straw along the center fold. Install a paper clip in the nose end of the straw. Adjust the leading edge slats and trim tabs as shown in the photograph.

TYPE: stretched delta
WINGSPAN: 4⅞"
LENGTH: 11"
WEIGHT: 4.2 grams

PILOT REPORT

This is a stretched delta that flies well at moderate speeds. Utilizing inverted twin vertical fins, this design flies like a typical delta.

MATERIALS REQUIRED

1 5″ × 8″ index card
1 plastic straw
1 paper clip
cellophane tape
ruler
razor blade

13A) Place the index card as shown.

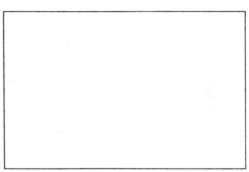

13B) Fold the card in half lengthwise.

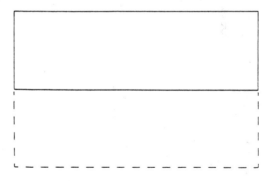

13C) Measure 1⅝″ from the top and ⅜″ from the nose. Cut along the diagonal line.

13D) Cut the twin rudders 1¼" as shown. Cut the trim tabs ½".

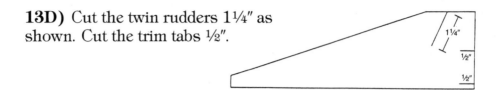

13E) Fold the twin rudders, noting the canted angle. Using the ruler, fold the leading edge slats ¼".

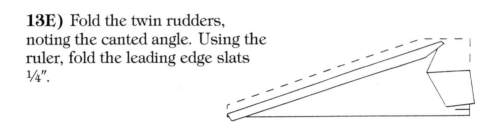

13F) Tape a straw 3" from the end of the trim tabs. Install a paper clip in the nose end of the straw. Adjust the wing dihedral and position the trim tab as shown in the photograph.

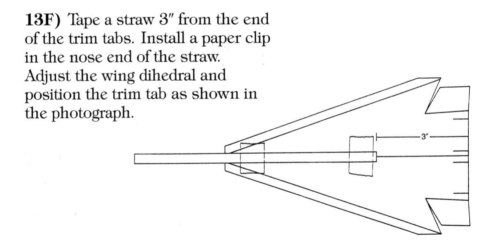

TYPE: square-tipped diamond
WINGSPAN: 8"
LENGTH: 9½"
WEIGHT: 5.3 grams

PILOT REPORT

I like this design a great deal. Very efficient, simple to build, and easy to fly, it is great indoors as well as outdoors. Two paper clips can be used indoors and three outdoors for better wind penetration.

MATERIALS REQUIRED

1 5″ × 8″ index card
1 plastic straw
2 or 3 paper clips
pencil
cellophane tape
ruler
razor blade

14A) Fold the index card in half crosswise.

14B) With the fold on the bottom, mark three measurements as shown: ⅝″, 1½″, and 2″.

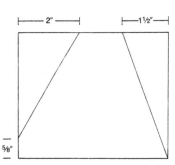

14C) Cut the upper corners off.

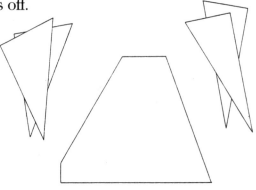

14D) Make two cuts, one ⅜″ and the other ⅝″ for the trim tabs. Using the ruler, fold the leading edge slats ⅜″.

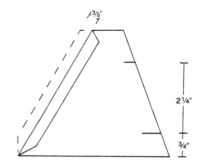

14E) From one of the larger triangles cut from the leading edge of the wing, fabricate a vertical fin by trimming the points as shown.

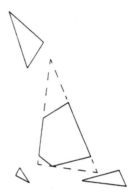

14F) Make a ¼″ cut through both sides of one end of the plastic straw. Cut two ¼″-wide strips of cellophane tape and use them to attach the vertical fin to the plane. Trim off any excess tape.

14G) Tape the wing to the bottom of the straw with the trailing edge point just touching the vertical fin. Attach two paper clips to the nose. (Use all three clips for outdoor flying.) Position the trim tabs as shown in the photo.

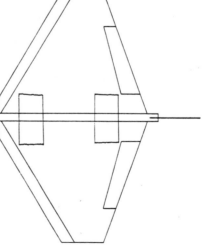

TYPE: delta
WINGSPAN: 8″
LENGTH: 7½″
WEIGHT: 4.8 grams

PILOT REPORT

This interesting design has an inverted V tail located under the trailing edge of the delta wing. It is basically the same as design #16, except for a slightly higher wing loading and the addition of winglets. This very sweet flying airplane is excellent for windy outdoor flying from a high launching point.

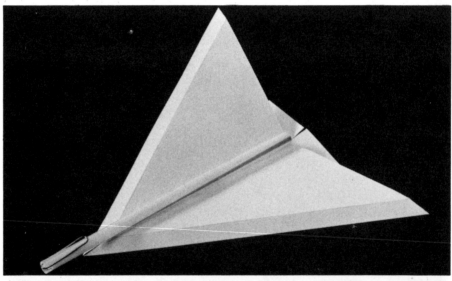

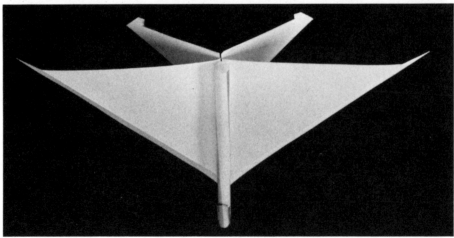

MATERIALS REQUIRED

2 5″ × 8″ index cards
1 plastic straw
1 paper clip
pencil
cellophane tape
ruler
razor blade

15A) Trace the full-size template on one of the index cards. Turn *the template over* and trace it again on the second card.

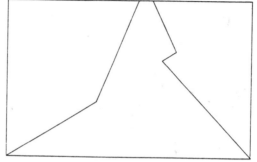

15B) Cut out the pattern.

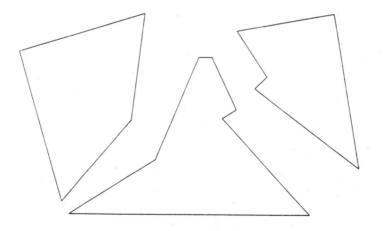

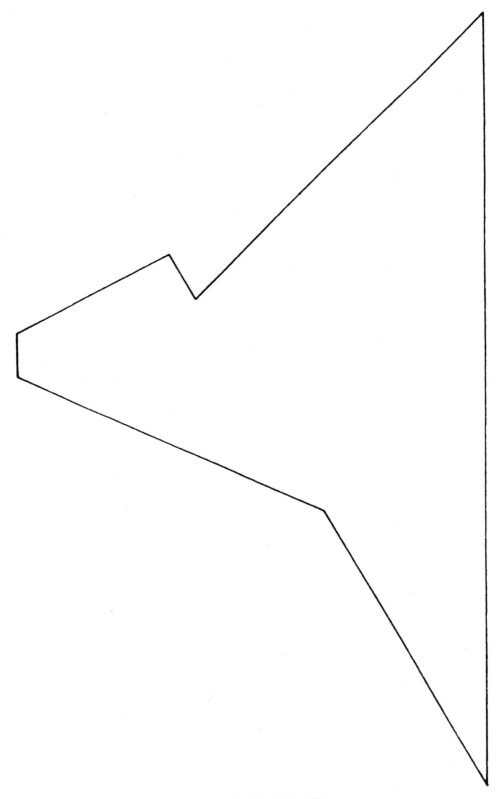

FULL-SIZE TEMPLATE

15C) Place the cutouts on top of each other. Make a ¼″ cut in the approximate position shown.

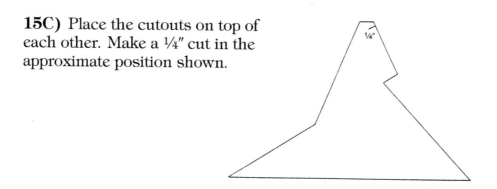

15D) Using the ruler, fold the stabilizer over onto the lined side. Fold the other cutout in the same manner.

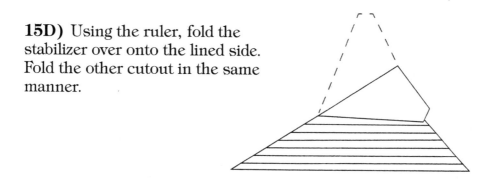

15E) Tape the two wing sections together as shown. (The lines on the cards are shown for clarity.) Tape on both sides.

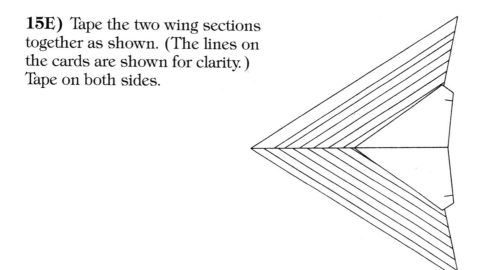

15F) Fold the trim tabs up to form a crease. Refold them slightly in the opposite direction. Cut approximately ¾" off the nose end of the wing.

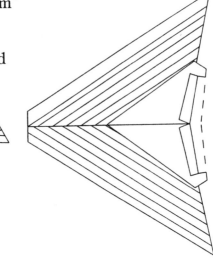

15G) Using the ruler, fold the leading edge slats ⅜".

15H) Trim the plastic straw down to 7". Tape the straw in the center of the wings. Attach a paper clip to the nose end of the straw. Position the slats and trim tabs as shown in the photo.

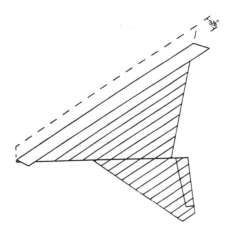

16

TYPE: delta with winglets
WINGSPAN: 6½″
LENGTH: 8⅜″
WEIGHT: 4.6 grams

PILOT REPORT

This design utilizes winglets, which make it slightly more efficient and more stable than #15. A great airplane.

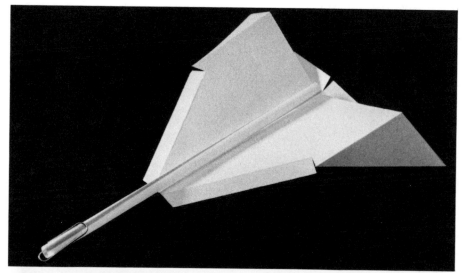

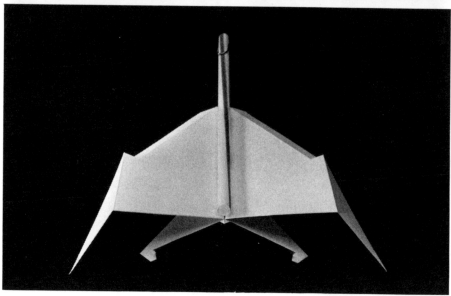

MATERIALS REQUIRED

2 5″×8″ index cards
1 plastic straw
1 paper clip
pencil
cellophane tape
ruler
razor blade

16A) Trace the pattern onto one of the index cards. *Turn the template over* and trace it on the second index card.

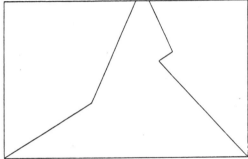

16B) Cut out the two patterns.

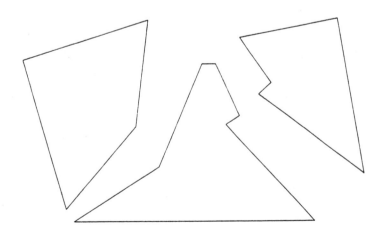

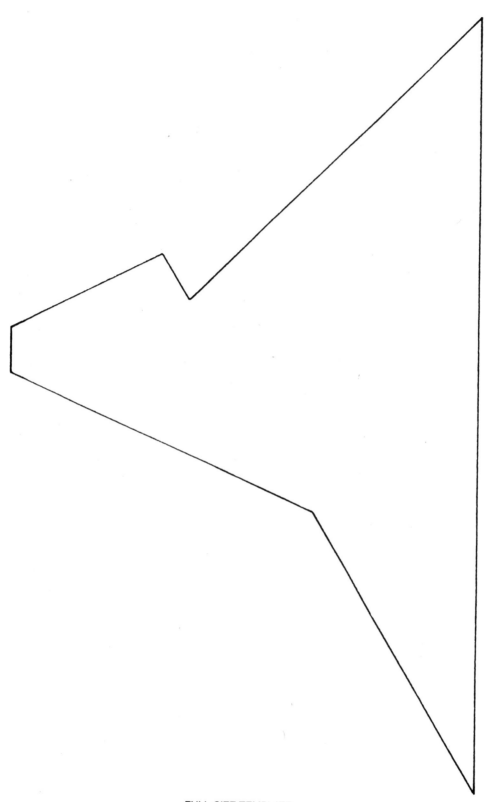

FULL-SIZE TEMPLATE

16C) Place the cutouts on top of each other. Make a ¼″ cut as shown.

16D) Using the ruler, fold the stabilizer over onto the lined side as shown. Fold the other cutout in the same manner.

16E) Tape the two wing sections together. (The lines on the cards are shown for clarity.) Tape on both sides.

16F) Fold the trim tabs up to form a crease. Refold the tabs slightly in the opposite direction. Cut approximately ¾″ off the nose end of the wing as shown.

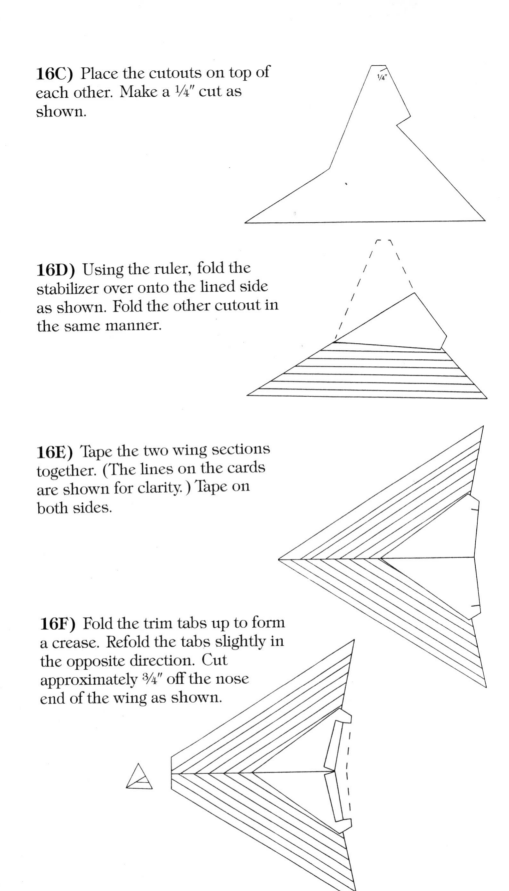

16G) On the trailing edge of the wing, measure 1½″ from the wingtip and fold the twin rudders down, noting the canted angle. Make a ⅜″ cut in the leading edge near the folded twin rudders as shown. (The lines on the card have been eliminated to highlight this area.)

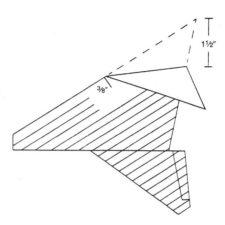

16H) Using the ruler, fold down the leading edge slats.

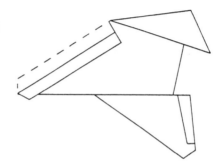

16I) Tape the plastic straw to the top of the wing. Add the paper clip to the nose. Position the leading edge slats and trim tabs as shown in the photograph.

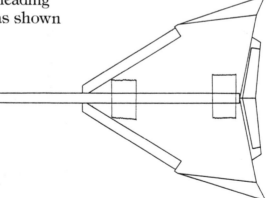

DESIGN *17*

TYPE: swept taper
WINGSPAN: 8″
LENGTH: 8″
WEIGHT: 2.8 grams

PILOT REPORT

This is a rather conventional design and configuration with the addition of an M tail. A great airplane for indoor flying at moderate speeds.

MATERIALS REQUIRED

1 5″ × 8″ index card
1 plastic straw
1 paper clip
pencil
cellophane tape
ruler
razor blade

17A) Fold the index card in half crosswise.

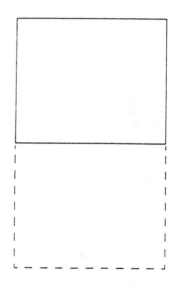

17B) Mark the measurements.

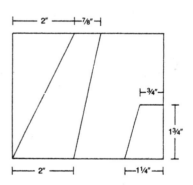

17C) Cut along the lines to produce a wing and tail.

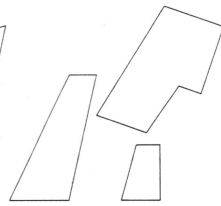

17D) Make two ¼" cuts on the tail section as shown. Make two cuts for wing flaps.

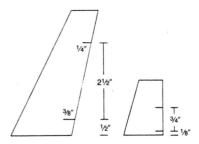

17E) Using the ruler, fold the leading edge slats ⅜" at the wingtip. Fold the wing flaps and the twin rudders at the 1" mark, noting the canted angle.

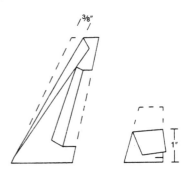

17F) Measure ³⁄₁₆" from the trailing edge of the tail and tape the tail to the bottom of the straw. Measure 2¾" from the nose of the straw and tape the wing underneath. Attach the paper clip to the nose end of the straw. Position the trim tabs as shown in the photo.

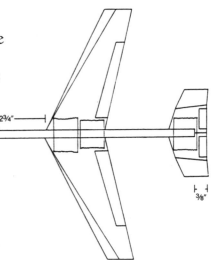

TYPE: swept taper
WINGSPAN: 8″
LENGTH: 8″
WEIGHT: 3.4 grams

PILOT REPORT

This design is similar to #17, but it has a more swept wing and a conventional tail. This airplane is good for indoor flying at moderate speeds.

MATERIALS REQUIRED

    1 5″ × 8″ index card
    1 plastic straw
    1 paper clip
    cellophane tape
    ruler
    razor blade

18A) Fold the index card in half widthwise.

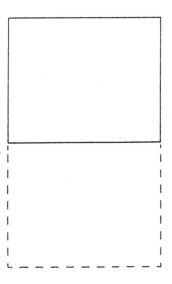

18B) With the fold on the bottom, cut out the wing section.

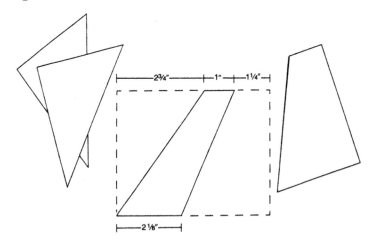

18C) Cut a stabilizer from the unused folded material. Make two ¼″ cuts on the stabilizer for trim tabs. Cut flaps in the wing as shown, ½″ cut inboard and ⅜″ cut at the wingtip.

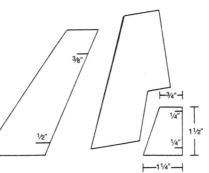

18D) Cut out a single vertical fin from scrap index card. Fold leading edge slats as shown.

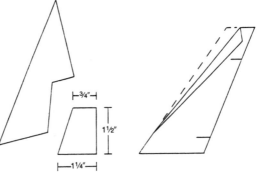

18E) With the stabilizer still folded, tape the vertical fin to the stabilizer on both sides. Trim off the excess tape.

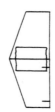

18F) Tape the stabilizer to the top of the straw. Tape the wing underneath the straw 2½″ back from the nose of the straw. Attach the paper clip to the nose of the straw. Position the slats, flaps, and trim tabs as shown in the photograph.

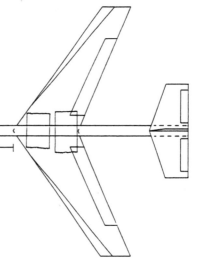

TYPE: constant cord
WINGSPAN: 6¾"
LENGTH: 8½"
WEIGHT: 5.3 grams

PILOT REPORT

This conventional design is good exposure for your business card. With this design's high wing loading, it flies well indoors and outdoors.

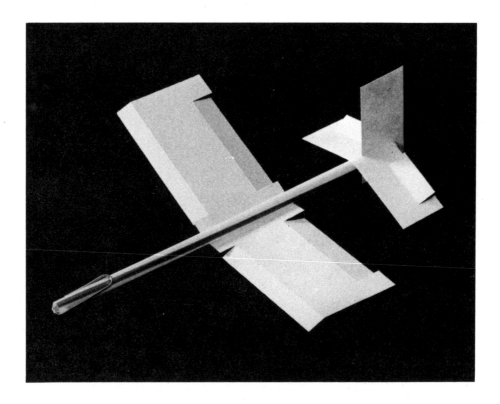

MATERIALS REQUIRED

    3 business cards
    1 plastic straw
    2 paper clips
    cellophane tape
    ruler
    razor blade
    5-minute epoxy glue
    sandpaper

19A) Tape the narrow ends of two business cards together. Trim off any excess tape. Cut the third business card in half lengthwise to form two 1"-wide strips.

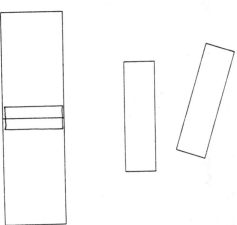

19B) Fold the wings along the taped joint. Fold one of the 1" strips as shown.

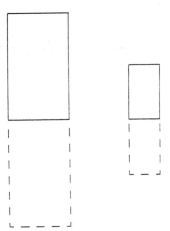

19C) Make ⅜″ cuts in the folded 1″ strip for trim tabs. Make ½″ cuts for flaps in the wing section. Make a ⅜″ cut on the leading edge of the wing.

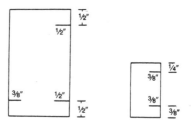

19D) Fold the leading edge slats on the main wing. Retrieve the other 1″ strip and trim it to a length of 2½″.

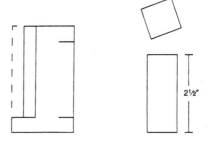

19E) Make a ⅜″ cut ¾″ from one end of the vertical fin. Make a ⅜″ cut on the folded line of the stabilizer between the trim tabs as shown (the center crease has been omitted for clarity).

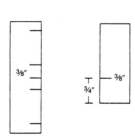

19F) Make a ¾″ cut in the end of a plastic straw. Insert the vertical fin at the cut in the stabilizer so a cross is formed. Use a few drops of 5-minute epoxy to affix the tail assembly to the straw. Lightly sand the straw with sandpaper in the contact area to ensure a good bond. Place the vertical fin through the cut in the straw. Three views—top, side, and front—are provided for clarity.

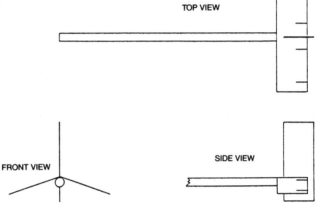

TOP VIEW

FRONT VIEW

SIDE VIEW

19G) Glue the wing under the straw 3⅜″ from the nose end of the straw. Position the flaps, leading edge slats, and trim tabs as shown in the photo. Attach the two paper clips to the nose end of the straw.

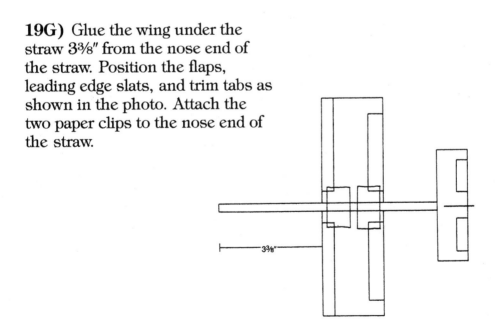

3⅜″

TYPE: tapered delta
WINGSPAN: 8″
LENGTH: 8½″
WEIGHT: 6.3 grams

PILOT REPORT

This design is unique in that the main wing is raised well above the straw. Use of a V tail for simplicity and light weight enhances performance. This design is great at low to moderate speeds.

MATERIALS REQUIRED

2 5″ × 8″ index cards
1 plastic straw
4 paper clips
pencil
cellophane tape
ruler
razor blade

20A) Fold one index card in half widthwise.

20B) Measure 3¼″ on the bottom fold and 1¼″ from the top and cut out along the diagonal line to create the wing.

1¼″

3¼″

20C) Measure 1½″ along the fold of the unused portion of the index card. Measure 3″ up from the fold and ¾″ horizontally. From this point cut the V tail.

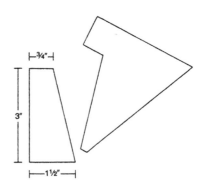

20D) Cut a strip 1½″ by 6″ from the second index card and fold in half as shown.

20E) Fold the tabs down approximately ⅝″ on the outside, noting the canted angle, which is important for proper wing incidence. Fold the other side in an exact mirror image.

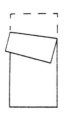

20F) Cut trim tabs on the V tail as shown. Cut flaps in the wing as shown. Fold back the leading edge slat on the wing approximately ½″.

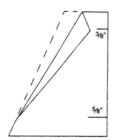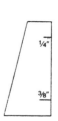

20G) Tape the V tail and wing struts to the straw. The wing strut leading edge is 3¾″ from the front of the straw. Note the canted angles of the wing strut tabs in the photograph.

3¾″

20H) On the underside of the wing draw two 1½″ lines parallel to the center fold. Tape the strut tabs to these lines. Adjust the wing anhedral, leading edge slats, flaps, V tail, and trim tabs as shown in the photograph. Attach the paper clips to the nose.

DESIGN *21*

TYPE: LEX taper
WINGSPAN: 8″
LENGTH: 5¼″
WEIGHT: 2.6 grams

PILOT REPORT

This is another personal favorite of mine. Not only does it fly well, but it looks great. A LEX taper wing with an inverted V tail group and strakes that extend under the wing produce a very stable and efficient design.

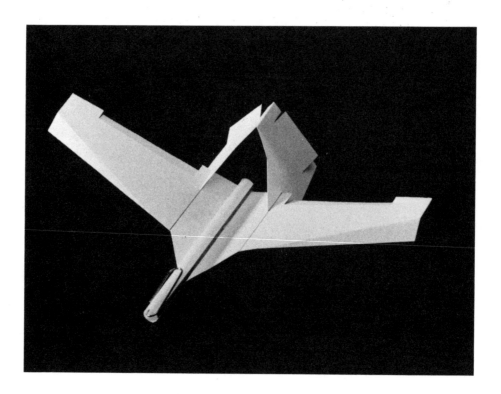

MATERIALS REQUIRED

1 5″ × 8″ index card
1 plastic straw
1 paper clip
pencil
cellophane tape
ruler
razor blade

21A) Fold the index card in half crosswise.

21B) Trace the full-size templates on the folded index card. Note that the folded end of the index card is toward you.

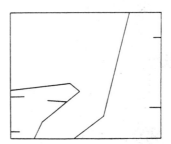

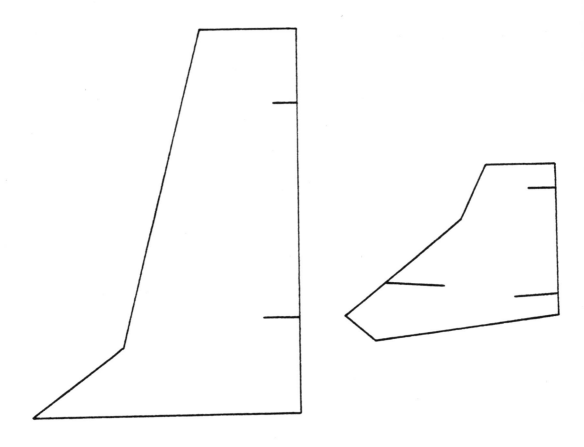

FULL-SIZE TEMPLATE

21C) Cut out the wing and tail section. Cut the trim tabs and optional flaps while the paper is folded. Make a ⅝″ cut in front of the trim tabs and widen the cut slightly so that the wing section will slide into it without twisting the tail.

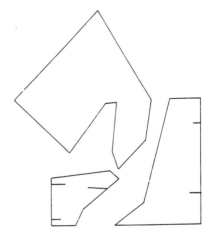

114

21D) Fold the flaps and leading edge slats ⅜″.

21E) Lay the wing flat and draw two parallel lines ¾″ from either side of the center fold.

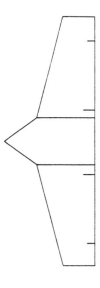

21F) With the tail in an inverted V position, slide the wing into the slots in line with the line you drew in the preceding step, and tape it in place. (The parallel lines have been eliminated from this drawing.)

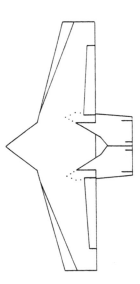

21G) Cut the plastic straw to a length of 4″. Tape the straw to the trailing edge of the wing. Position the flaps (optional), leading edge slats, dihedral, and trim tabs as shown in the photograph. Attach a paper clip to the nose.

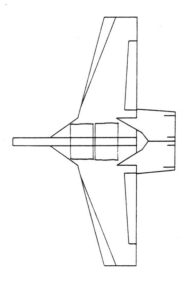

22

TYPE: tapered swept
WINGSPAN: 8"
LENGTH: 6 ½"
WEIGHT: 2.8 grams

PILOT REPORT

This clean design flies as well as looks good. Very stable, it is great for indoor as well as outdoor flying at moderate speeds. Of interest is the slight tail wagging that occurs in flight. This is due to the horizontal stabilizer riding in the turbulent slipstream of the wing.

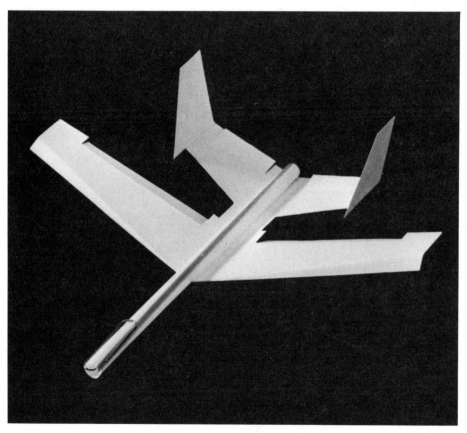

MATERIALS REQUIRED

1 5″ × 8″ index card
1 plastic straw
1 paper clip
pencil
cellophane tape
ruler
razor blade

22A) Fold the index card in half crosswise.

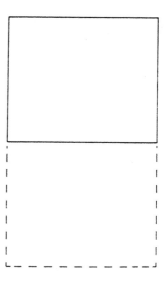

22B) Trace the full size template onto the folded index card.

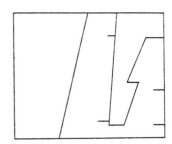

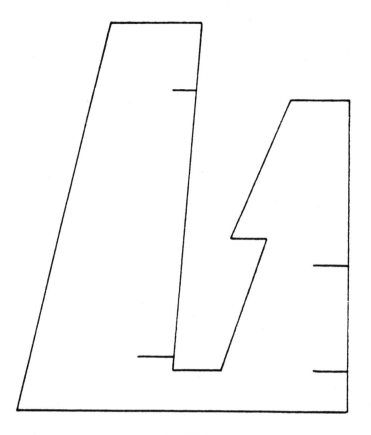

FULL-SIZE TEMPLATE

22C) Cut out the pattern and make the flaps (optional). Do not cut the trim tabs yet.

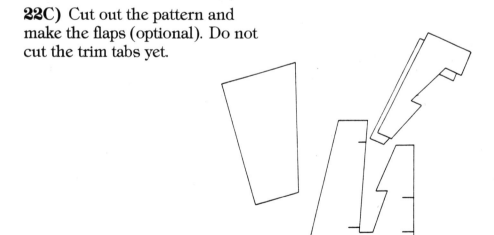

22D) Fold the twin vertical fins parallel as shown.

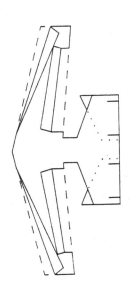

22E) Unfold the airplane at the middle and lay it on a flat surface with the twin vertical fins underneath. Using the ruler, fold the flaps and leading edge slats as shown. Now cut the trim tabs.

22F) Cut the plastic straw to a length of 6 ⅜"(this is a critical measure), and tape the straw as shown. Attach the paper clip to the nose. Position the trim tabs, vertical fins, and optional flaps as shown in the photograph.

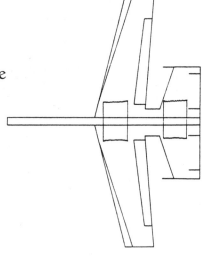

TYPE: swept
WINGSPAN: 7"
LENGTH: 8 ⅛"
WEIGHT: 3.7 grams

PILOT REPORT

This design has its wingtips fixed to the horizontal stabilizer, creating a very strong airframe. It utilizes winglets that also act as vertical fins enhancing lift and stability. Good in the moderate speed range for indoor as well as outdoor flying.

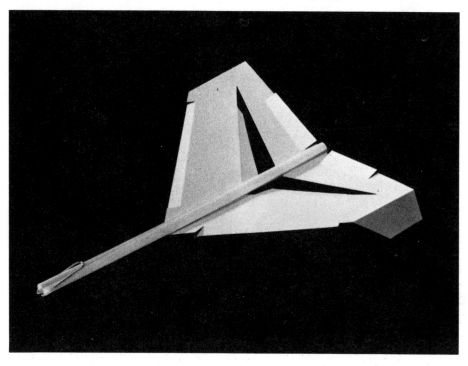

1 5″ × 8″ index card
1 plastic straw
1 paper clip
cellophane tape
ruler
razor blade

23A) Place the index card in the position shown.

23B) Fold the card in half widthwise.

23C) Measure 1″ from the top right and cut on a diagonal line to the lower left corner.

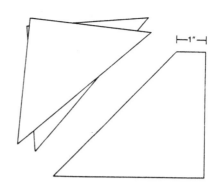

23D) Cut a pie slice out of the folded end.

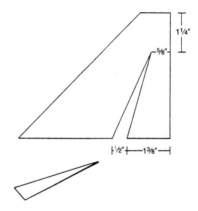

23E) Using the ⅝″ dimension as a guideline, cut the flaps. Cut the trim tabs ⁵⁄₁₆″. Cut the leading edge slats as shown.

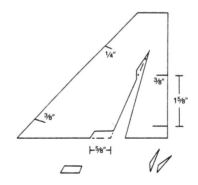

23F) Fold twin rudders approximately ¾″. Fold back the leading edge slats.

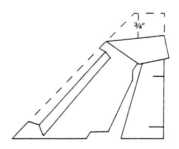

23G) Tape the straw onto the wing center line as shown. Attach the paper clip to the nose. Position the leading edge slats, flaps, and trim tabs as shown in the photograph.

TYPE: swept flying wing
WINGSPAN: $8''$
LENGTH: $5''$
WEIGHT: 2.5 grams

PILOT REPORT

This flying wing design is extremely efficient. The entire airframe provides lift, since it has no load-carrying plastic straw or tail surfaces. This design doesn't even have a vertical fin; it uses the wingtip vortex drag for yaw stability. A great flier for indoor use in the moderate speed range.

MATERIALS REQUIRED

   1 5″ × 8″ index card
2 paper clips
pencil
ruler
razor blade

24A) Fold the index card in half crosswise.

24B) Mark the measurements and draw lines as shown.

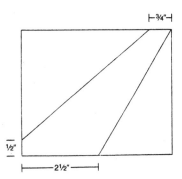

24C) Cut along the lines.

24D) Make a ½″ cut and a ⅜″ cut to the dimensions shown for trim tabs.

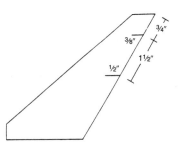

24E) Using the ruler, fold the leading edge slats over ¼″.

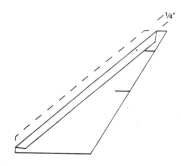

24G) Unfold the wing. Fold the trim tabs as shown in the photograph. Attach the two paper clips to the nose.

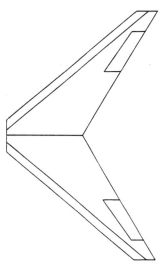

25

TYPE: canard
WINGSPAN: $7\frac{1}{8}''$
LENGTH: $8\frac{1}{4}''$
WEIGHT: 10.2 grams

PILOT REPORT

With eight business cards, this design is literally a flying billboard.

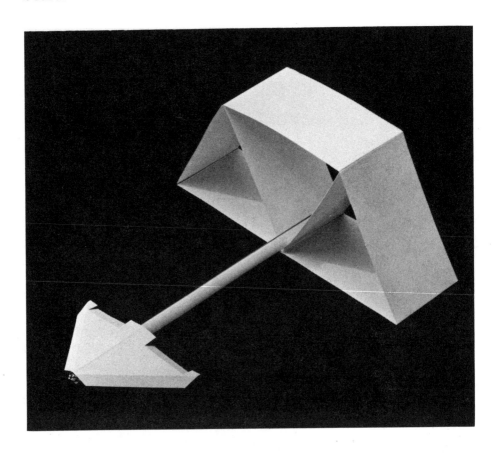

MATERIALS REQUIRED

8 business cards
1 plastic straw
3 paper clips
cellophane tape
ruler
razor blade

25A) Join and tape two strips of three business cards end to end as shown. Tape only on one side.

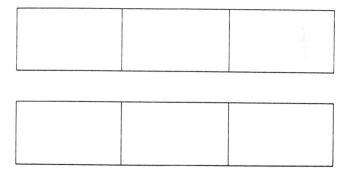

25B) Stand the cards on edge and tape them into two triangles as shown.

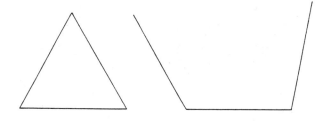

25C) Position the two triangles together and join them at two points with tape. Tape another whole business card to the other two triangle points.

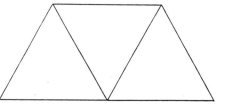

25D) Fold the last business card in half crosswise.

25E) Cut the corners off as shown.

25F) Using the ruler, fold the leading edge slats ¼".

25G) Cut the trim tabs as shown.

25H) Tape the front wing to the straw. Tape the straw into the center notch of the business card/wing assembly. Fold the canard trim tabs down. Attach 3 paper clips to the nose as shown in the photograph.

TYPE: canard
WINGSPAN: 3½"
LENGTH: 8½"
WEIGHT: 2.5 grams

PILOT REPORT

You'll really like this cruise missile design. It is very stable and very fast. This airplane really flies only in the moderate- to fast-speed range.

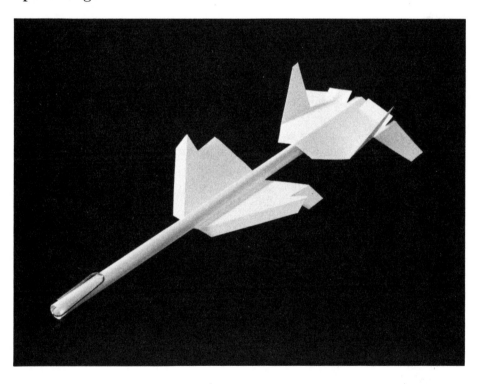

MATERIALS REQUIRED

2 business cards
1 plastic straw
1 paper clip
cellophane tape
ruler
razor blade

26A) Fold two business cards in half lengthwise.

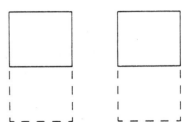

26B) Cut the corners off as shown.

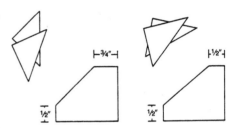

26C) To make the front wing, fold the leading edge slat ³⁄₁₆″ using the ruler. Cut and fold the winglet ⁵⁄₁₆″, noting the canted angle.

26D) To make the rear wing, cut and fold the twin vertical fins ⁷⁄₈″, noting the canted angle.

26E) Make two ¼″ cuts ¾″ apart for trim tabs on the rear wing.

26F) Fold the rear wing in half backwards and fold the top twin vertical fins. Note the canted angle.

26G) Tape the front wing to the bottom of the straw 3½″ from the nose. Place the trim tabs and vertical fins in the approximate positions shown in the photograph. Attach the paper clip to the nose.

TYPE: triplane
WINGSPAN: 8″
LENGTH: 8″
WEIGHT: 4 grams

PILOT REPORT

This is a "triplane" using a lifting canard in the nose, a conventional taper wing, and an M tail surface. Aviation seems to go in phases, much like clothing fashions. This "triplane" arrangement is the current rage. This design is excellent for indoor as well as outdoor flying at moderate speeds.

MATERIALS REQUIRED

1 5″×8″ index card
1 plastic straw
2 paper clips
pencil
cellophane tape
ruler
razor blade

27A) Fold the index card in half crosswise.

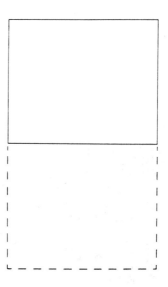

27B) Trace the full-size templates onto the folded index card.

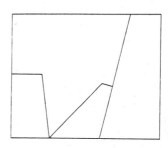

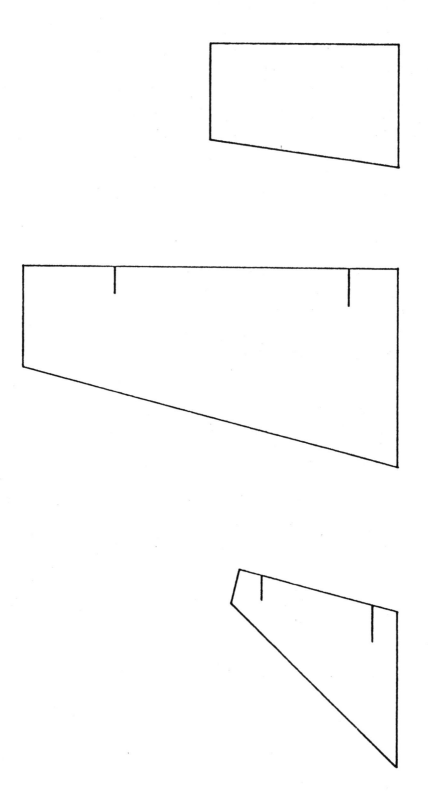

FULL-SIZE TEMPLATE

27C) Cut out the wing, canard foreplane, and tail section.

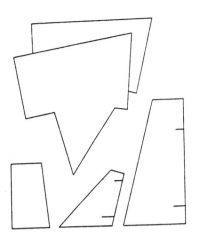

27D) Fold the trim tabs on the canard, using the ruler. Fold the leading edge slats approximately ¼″ at the wingtip. Fold the flaps on the main wing. Fold the tail fins, noting the canted angle.

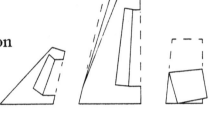

27E) Using the 3½″ measurement, tape the canard foreplane, wing, and the M tail to the straw. Refer to the photograph for clarity. Use the razor blade to reopen the flaps if necessary.

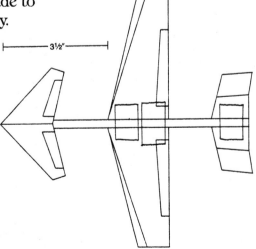

3½″

28

TYPE: F/A 18 Hornet-LEX delta
WINGSPAN: 6¼"
LENGTH: 8"
WEIGHT: 4.1 grams

PILOT REPORT

This design is almost foolproof to make. The performance is also excellent. The wing and tail surfaces of airplanes #28, #29, and #30 are in the same scale, but there is a difference in their overall size and design. Except for the fuselage, these designs are faithful reproductions of real fighter planes.

paper or tracing paper
2 5″×8″ index cards
1 paper clip
pencil
cellophane tape
ruler
razor blade

28A) Fold the index card in half lengthwise.

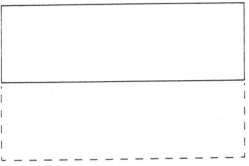

28B) Transfer the full-size templates onto a sheet of paper or tracing paper. Then trace that pattern onto the folded index card. Be sure the fold is on the bottom as shown.

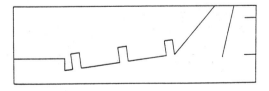

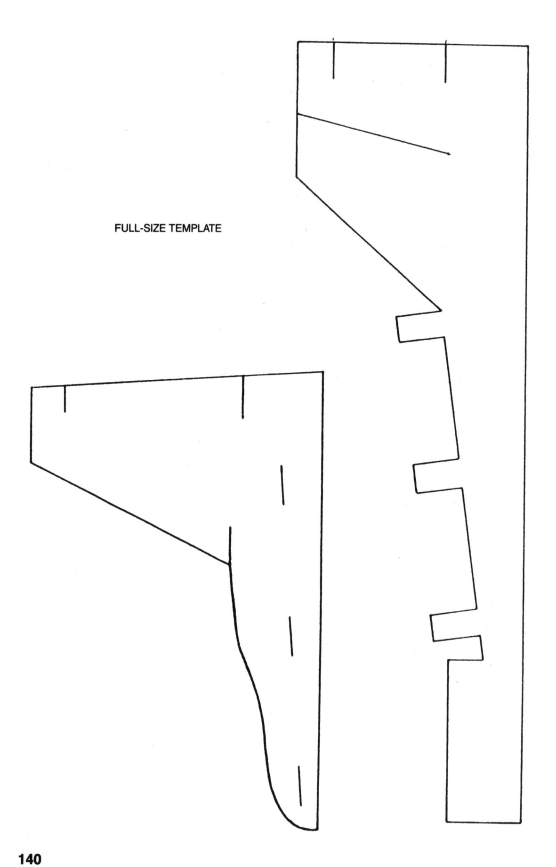

FULL-SIZE TEMPLATE

28C) Cut out the fuselage section.

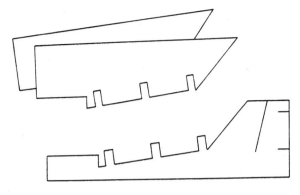

28D) Fold the second index card in half crosswise.

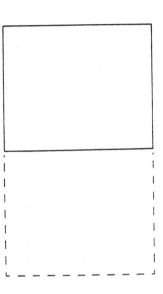

28E) Trace the full-size wing template onto the second folded index card.

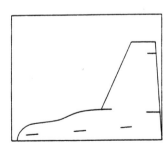

28F) Cut out the wing section.

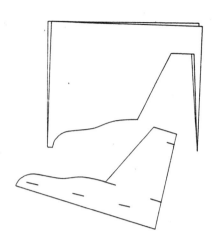

28G) Using the ruler, fold the leading edge slats and flaps. Cut the three ⅜″ wing-attach slots. Insert the blade and wiggle it slightly to open up the slots.

28H) At the base of the cut and at the rearmost tab, on this canted angle, fold the twin vertical fins and stabilizers up. Fold nose tabs as shown.

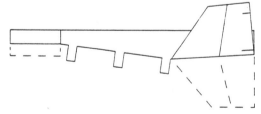

28I) Insert the fuselage tabs into the wing slots and fold the tabs over. Tape them in place as shown in the bottom view.

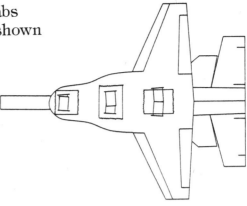

28J) Position the wing dihedral, stabilizer anhedral, leading edge slats, flaps, twin vertical fins, and trim tabs as shown in the front view and the photograph. Attach the paper clip to the nose.

DESIGN 29

TYPE: F 15 Eagle-LEX delta
WINGSPAN: 5⅞"
LENGTH: 8¾"
WEIGHT: 4.3 grams

PILOT REPORT

Like designs #28 and #30, this is a very stable airplane that is terrific for indoor as well as outdoor flying in the moderate-speed range.

3 5″×8″ index cards
1 paper clip
pencil
cellophane tape
ruler
razor blade

29A) Fold the index card in half lengthwise.

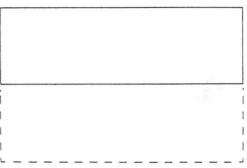

29B) Trace the full-size fuselage template onto the folded index card. Be sure that the fold is at the bottom.

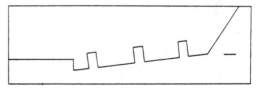

29C) Cut out the fuselage section.

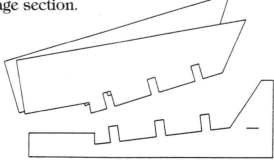

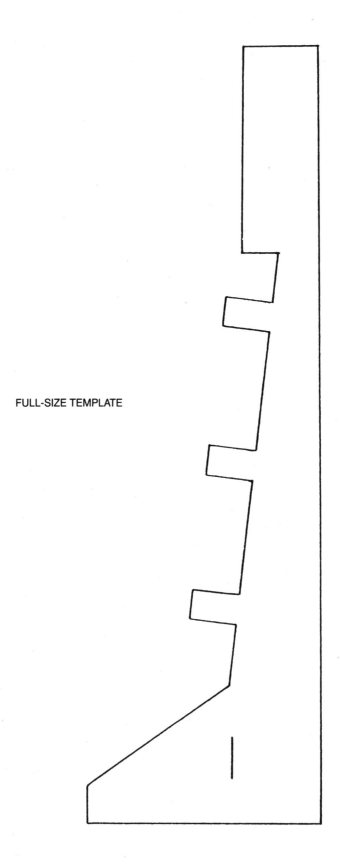

FULL-SIZE TEMPLATE

29D) Fold the second index card in half crosswise.

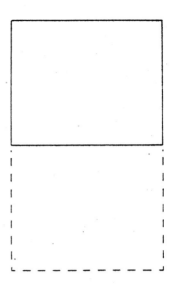

29E) Trace the full-size wing template onto the second folded index card. Be sure to trace the wing slots.

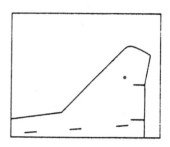

29F) Cut out the wing section. Cut the ⅜″ wing-attach slots and flaps. Fold the leading edge slats as shown.

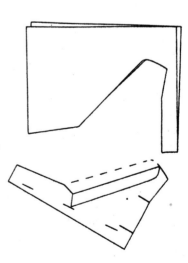

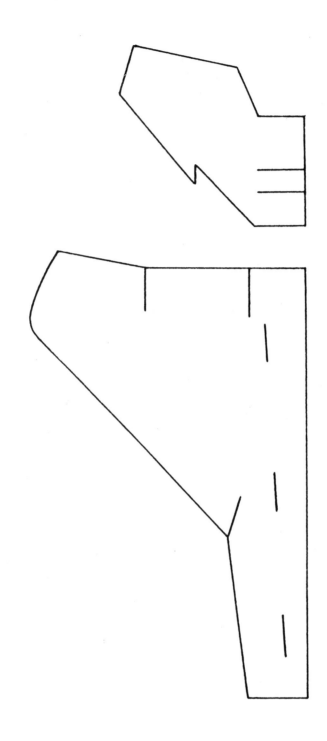

FULL-SIZE TEMPLATE

29G) Fold in half the scrap left over from the wing section. With the fold on the bottom, trace the full-size stabilizer template. Be sure to include the mounting tabs.

29H) Cut out the stabilizer.

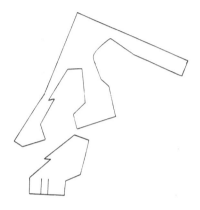

29I) Unfold the stabilizer and lay it flat. Make a ¼" cut along the center fold and fold the mounting tabs as shown.

29J) Fold the twin fins up. Fold the nose section up.

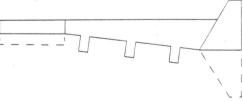

29K) Refold and tape the nose section into a triangle as shown in the bottom view. Insert the fuselage tabs into the wing slots. Fold the tabs over toward each other and tape. Trim the front two tabs to ⅜". Mount the stabilizer by inserting the two tabs into the two slots at the base of the twin vertical fins. Tape the tabs to the inside surface of the vertical fins.

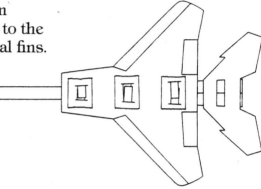

29L) Position the flaps, leading edge slats, and vertical fins in the approximate position shown in the front view and in the photograph. Attach the paper clip to the nose.

TYPE: F 20 Tigershark-LEX delta
WINGSPAN: 4⅝"
LENGTH: 8"
WEIGHT: 3.2 grams

PILOT REPORT

This is a faithful miniature of the jet fighter that Chuck Yeager flies in the soft drink commercial. It has a higher wing loading than designs #28 and #29. This enables it to fly better outdoors in the wind. Of all the designs in this book, this is my personal favorite.

MATERIALS REQUIRED

2 5"×8" index cards
1 paper clip
pencil
cellophane tape
ruler
razor blade

30A) Fold both index cards in half lengthwise.

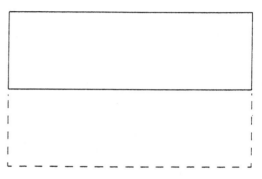

30B) Trace the full-size template on one folded index card, making sure the fold is on the bottom.

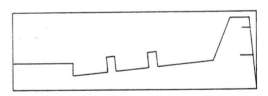

30C) Cut out the fuselage section.

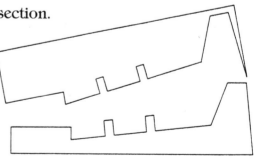

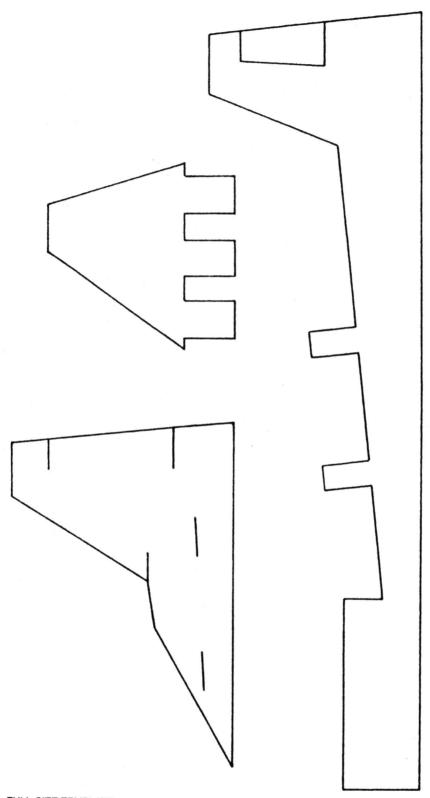

FULL-SIZE TEMPLATE

30D) Trace the full-size template of the wing and vertical fin onto the second folded index card.

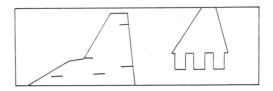

30E) Cut out the wing and vertical fin. You will end up with two fins; put one away to use in the future. Cut the two ⅜" wing-attach slots. Wiggle the razor blade to open up these slots slightly.

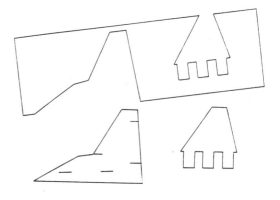

30F) Fold the horizontal stabilizers as shown, noting the canted angle. Fold the flaps and leading edge slats as shown.

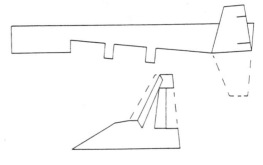

30G) Unfold the fuselage and lay it flat with the crease down. Cut 1⅞″ along the center fold, ⅛″ from the trailing edge as shown in the side view of step 36H. (The center fold line has been omitted from this drawing for clarity.) Fold the nose tabs toward the center crease.

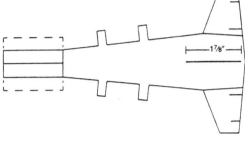

30H) Fold the fore and aft tabs of the vertical fin to one side; fold the middle tab to the other side. Slide the vertical fin from underneath and, using as little tape as possible, tape the tabs to the inside of the fuselage. (Look at step 30I for the bottom view). Fold the nose tabs to form a triangular tube. Tape them in place. (Refer to step 30J for a front view.)

30I) Insert the four fuselage tabs into the four wing slots. Fold the tabs over and tape them as shown in the bottom view.

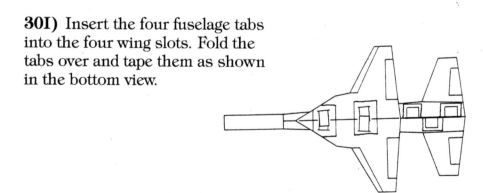

30J) Position the wing dihedral and the stabilizer anhedral as shown in the front view. Position the flaps, slats, and trim tabs as shown in the photograph. Attach the paper clip to the nose.

Peter Vollheim is president of two manufacturing firms. When not at work, he frequently flies his home-built Glasair for pleasure or in New England–area airshows. He lives in southern New Hampshire with his wife and son.